I0767294

BLANK PAGE
FOR YOUR CONVENIENCE

BLANK PAGE
FOR YOUR CONVENIENCE

BLANK PAGE
FOR YOUR CONVENIENCE

BLANK PAGE
FOR YOUR CONVENIENCE

BLANK PAGE
FOR YOUR CONVENIENCE

BLANK PAGE
FOR YOUR CONVENIENCE

BLANK PAGE
FOR YOUR CONVENIENCE

BLANK PAGE
FOR YOUR CONVENIENCE

BLANK PAGE
FOR YOUR CONVENIENCE

BLANK PAGE
FOR YOUR CONVENIENCE

BLANK PAGE
FOR YOUR CONVENIENCE

BLANK PAGE
FOR YOUR CONVENIENCE

BLANK PAGE
FOR YOUR CONVENIENCE

BLANK PAGE
FOR YOUR CONVENIENCE

**BLANK PAGE**
**FOR YOUR CONVENIENCE**

BLANK PAGE
FOR YOUR CONVENIENCE

BLANK PAGE
FOR YOUR CONVENIENCE

BLANK PAGE
FOR YOUR CONVENIENCE

BLANK PAGE
FOR YOUR CONVENIENCE

BLANK PAGE
FOR YOUR CONVENIENCE

BLANK PAGE
FOR YOUR CONVENIENCE

BLANK PAGE
FOR YOUR CONVENIENCE

BLANK PAGE
FOR YOUR CONVENIENCE

BLANK PAGE
FOR YOUR CONVENIENCE

BLANK PAGE
FOR YOUR CONVENIENCE

BLANK PAGE
FOR YOUR CONVENIENCE

BLANK PAGE
FOR YOUR CONVENIENCE

BLANK PAGE
FOR YOUR CONVENIENCE

BLANK PAGE
FOR YOUR CONVENIENCE

BLANK PAGE
FOR YOUR CONVENIENCE

# COLOR TESTER CHART

# COLOR TESTER CHART

THANK YOU!
We appreciate you for purchasing our product. We hope you had fun.
Please stay tuned for our next project coming soon from Magic Pen.